...are beauty inducers

our bodies
...are beauty inducers

j/j hastain

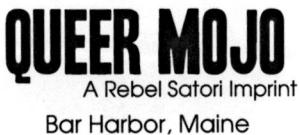

A Rebel Satori Imprint
Bar Harbor, Maine

REBEL SATORI PRESS
P.O. Box 363
Hulls Cove, ME 04644
www.rebelsatori.com

This is a creative work. Names, characters, places, and incidents are the product of the author's imagination and are used fictitiously and any resemblance to actual persons, living or dead, business establishments, events, or locales is entirely coincidental. The publisher does not have any control over and does not assume any responsibility for author or third-party websites or their content.

Copyright © 2010 by j/j hastain. All rights reserved. Except for brief passages quoted in newspaper, magazine, radio, television, or online reviews, no part of this book may be reproduced in any form or any means, electronic or mechanical, including photocopying, recording, or information or retrieval system, without the permission in writing from the publisher. Please do not participate in or encourage piracy of copyrighted materials in violation of the author's rights. Purchase only authorized editions.

Book design by Sven Davisson

Photography by j/j hastain

ISBN: 978-1-60864-012-6

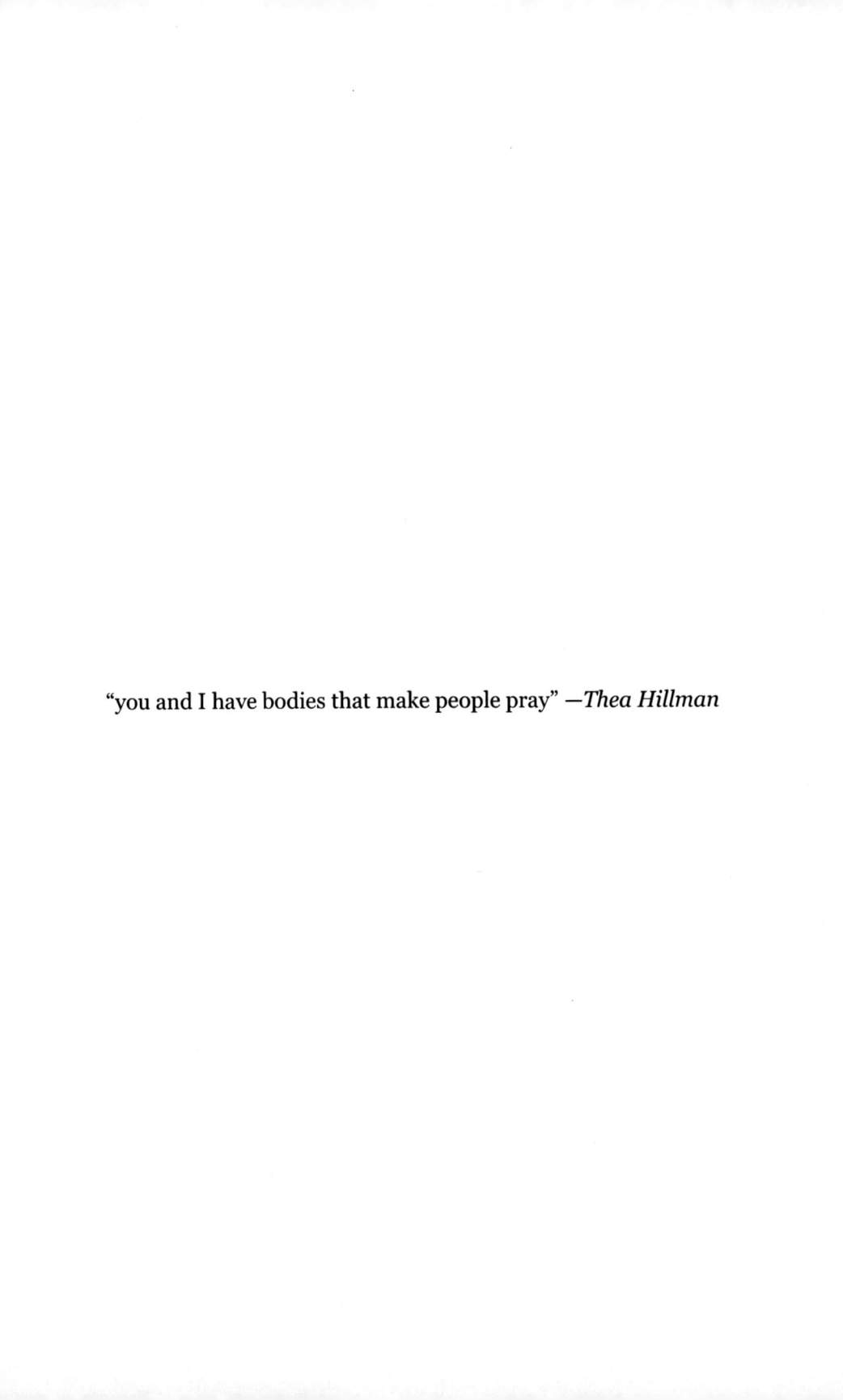

"you and I have bodies that make people pray" —*Thea Hillman*

our bodies are beauty inducers

pressure on two ends
        (even if those ends are not linearly connected)

    generates a further pressure

        which is the origin of the arc

motile-locations as a way to explore plenum
    as activism

    this is the embodiment of awe

        in ways that have never before been embodied

    this is the work of co-inhabiting non-debatable fullness

this is amorousness that is continuously morphing

on the levels of the meta

on the levels of the macro

altering shape and pressure   producing phantasmagoria

this is meat as it is becoming meat

through non-consecutive and non-chronological enactments

of girth and image

through relentless   withhold-less

sites and sounds of love

thermo-mimetic inks
    and ulterior genders

        these clandestine nutrients for a non-dualist future

I am interested in what can exist as prolonged scripture inside of a
    fossa or a gap

I am interested in new methods of touch   that emphasize
    patriarchy as obsolete

    this is the effort to reveal

        this is emotional-surgery

        this is the application of deep authenticities

    wherein body becomes a collaborative image
        for our ongoing forms to move through

::

integral sockets left in heaps along the roadside

::

somehow becoming reclaimed

and from there all embodiments are to be regarded

                                                                as past and future lives
                                            simultaneously

                there is a language

                      (or a set of languages)

                              for every embodiment

            to amplify the conjunctions in any fatigued throat
            and emerge with a new bold phrase

      therefore these languages of dark-turnip   and hybridity

        therefore the marrow of an always contemporary sex

we

      we are complex spherical unions   we are direct outlets

lifting into other dimensions through our sweat

            of amber   of "how much"

               of ample

           this is how   what once existed as a boundary

                begins to be integrated

           patiently always patiently awaiting

                  and proclaiming

the swells and dwellings of each of the aspects

               of this never before paginated

poetics of spill

(

      a story   of sensual math that redeems us

            these are the sultry caves that are the insides of the inside

         as both mortality and immortality are superimposed

           and our bodies are configured re-configured

                      through one another

I hold you in

beneath the blackening

clarity

you hold me heaving

"is your heart ok my Beloved"

      'yes warm and wide   warm and widening'

we are inventing ways to contact eternity
through sensation

      through reverie so lush   it is its own ecosystem

          always shifting and ever incapable of end

engaging with vigor and voraciousness

rather than diminution withholding or fear

        we begin to be recognized as a new type of history

        the body coming exquisitely undone

                how this is somehow a delicate alternate to mourning

may we always forcibly co-deteriorate and forgive

    the inapplicable or incorrect layers as we build

        for we have been given no model for the fusion of our bodies

                            yet we continue

    "we have been given no reprieve   nothing to emulate"

                          yet we continue

may we irrevocably feed our sedimentary shadowy joy

through the looms and portals of our own concoction

    may we

        may we

'I know my body   and it is incomplete   without you

I vow to vulnerably give my body to you'

tangibility is one of the most prominent   essential factors   of this life
because once you and I pass the threshold of death

    who knows if in our ultimate unbridled wisdom
                  we will choose to come back again in bodies
    let alone these specific bodies

'I want to know and adore and saturate   this body   your body
my body   as our deepest project'

chanting into one another's mouths

bleating lockets for a centrifugal jolt
          that leads us into new types of center

        new types of heart   new types of octave

    we imagine an amethyst the size of a shed

    filled with all of our amatory anatomies and totems

the utter enlock of each bleating clot

()

we bring the bleeding in like wind   through rituals

I hold you firm   into me

gently stripping your nipples   squeezing your body
                                              into pulpy loops

                this to harvest   entirely open doors

"please please make me come"

we begin sewing the eternity sign

needle and thread   into the skin   above my heart   then
    yours   then mine
then

       this is the rite from which all newness is generated

       a multi-account of our inked nadir

but more bold
more fisted

more vulnerable

                 more candelabra

              sticky with its indelible moments
              of opera

)(

I am rubbing your budding   bulges   as you slowly open
    your legs   more and more widely
you shake and brim with color

the reds that come through my hands into you   like puddles
beginning to spread across

your neck
as you come   I chant the milk of us

into your mouth eyes and ears

so exquisite as you thank me   calling me by my many names
    weeping as I suck   and swallow

and am covered in the country of our tears

countless and without end
as a pressure that demands

      "you are endless in me amazing   more than
      anything I have ever felt

        thank you for taking me so far in
          you are my tides

          you make me increased capacity   in me"

like photographs of a buoy
    or the multi-dimensional songs of stellar capitulations

        along this coven of refined and refining
        softs

rounding and rendering the glottal stops into curvatures

that this type of sensual vibrancy   is timeless content

and as the mirror breaks   it leaks our shared

morphing minutia into cosmos

no mannequins here

all mortar and altar

all lather and lace

warm interior contents

and sanctuaries of pact

enigma-city
00

we realize that there is no opposite to flesh

slow and languorous   the blood becoming solidified

        'I give you all of my breakage
            my capacity to trill'

there is an unconditional aching
        as we make love amidst the quotidian

surpassing that noise through our noise

        all of the things that there are no synonyms for

        velvet ribbons being tied around

        then hefty buttocks

        like peaches

        in a monk's hot

            flickering hands

these are the images of an always dripping inquiry

       these are drenched time

"I want you to sink your prick   deep into me
make me disclose

      turn me into vertical homophony

        I want to float in your grip

            as my prominent sea of color and non-dilution"

hearth

'I belong nowhere but in you'

      heir to   this erotic staple

        screaming squires of saturation

            becoming unencumbered light

skin quaking   affecting terra and all of its dyed parts

    "from behind"

I am clutching your body   pulling me into you
hardest muscle inside

    "I want to feel you from the inside"

        'then always articulate me as your inferno

            as your clutch'

    mercilessly   we crack open cliché

through erecting motions that enact an evolution of Adam and Eve

    as concept   as body

'circumvent me

    become   me'

    invocations of an increased

        mystery tilling corporeal

OO(

    you spoke to me in a voice   like a theorem I had once known
                                                                         in the space of my dreams

a theorem wherein I first understood pi as literal more than figurative
                pi   as the feeling of collected perfect pearls

                being sewn into the fleshy portions of skin
                just above my genitals

in this voice you said "I want you to know that the answer is yes
that I will give you anything you want
how does that make you feel?"

      and my   'dizzy   grateful   confident
      like I am truly home in you in us   it makes me feel

            extremely aroused relieved   and entirely ready'

it had to do with the way that you stopped me at the threshold of the
    door to the bedroom

and kissed me   longer than I kissed you   the way
    you held me there

total enrapture

'this is a demand   an omen of what is to come'

        then later you smiled smoothly
              as I read to you of memory and of cream

this was a scene that was noticeably spring   ripe   and blustering

   'my angel   I want you to settle into your body
      silky and swell   let yourself come entirely home

   as I show you were home really is'

how when we arrived in the city
            I pulled the car over to photograph the ladder
            that was protruding up to the sky

        you looked at a menu as I did this

upon getting back in the car you looked at the photos and exclaimed

   "this is what we've been talking about baby
      the ladder that leads to nowhere"

   'which is the same as saying the ladder that leads to everywhere'

prismatic-hinge

   and a stammering

we ordered shrimp
   you   a sensual wine me a salt bloody mary with extra chile vodka

      and we discussed

      drawing on the tablecloth

        illustrating sexualities and midi pots

        illustrating new modes for a conglomerate

you pulled a small kaleidoscope out of your purse and gave it to me

you then pulled out a top and spun it on the face of the table

'you are amazing how to you get it to spin so long and steady'

"I am good at twirling things between my fingers"

and we look
and we look

and we pant

    I gave you a letter that I had written that day
                            a letter to our eros
  a letter to you

      you dropped it down your shirt and it rested there
      an ecstatic map

I was then reminded of the conversation we had had earlier when I told you that your legs are my favorite complicated cartography

      I told you as I fed you garlic spinach
                that I would like the shape of our night to be

        'overtly   effeminate   admixture'
you walked into the room   heavy on me   let me watch you
                                                              "take off your clothes"

then as you climbed over to me   the light in the room dilating

you rolled me over and kissed my sides   with fervent pressure
with command of the languages of my body as if they were your
    languages of origin

leaving a gorgeous mark on the place where those two regions overlap

    I moaned   you moaned   this joint-knowledge of how much
                                                      those markings mean to me

    then you were kissing my mouth   rubbing your hands lightly
        over my gaping

                                        careful to touch and not touch

creating this aching   this longing
and I noticed I was capitulating   you felt the quivers intensify
    as you rolled me in your hands   taking me with such intention

    "told you I was good at rolling things between my fingers"

    luminous   entirely luminous

    'I will submit to you   do you like it when I submit to you?'

my body arching now

    "yeah   you arc for me   you let me see you
        let me hold you   let me know you
                you have the most beautiful body I have ever seen

            you are   perfect"

'I need you to make me exposed   like old growth forests
      like the bible being drowned'

    "but you are so wet my baby   you are so wild and hard and wet"

'I want more   I need more   more wet
                            wet that leads to a slow stretch'

you opened the lubricant and poured
the release in this   my body becoming an actual bios system
        how I could see the elements that populate me

in color stains   relevant streaks across some surface that
        stretched from
my childhood understanding of what happens to the desert in a flash
        flood
            to the way that a sea is capable of devouring entire vessels

you began by slowly moving your body over the lower half of my body
        so that I was holding onto you   gripping your ass
    with tenacity and tenuous
                                        with desperation

strobing and deep rubbing
        amongst all of that sureness   and my eyes began to close
which meant ceremony

        it meant having arrived at the place where a great
                            and immanent mercy

                            coadunates with my desire

it meant having arrived in the chamber

        'this is the definition of primal cascade'

"I don't think that's enough for you   you need more don't
    you baby"

    'yes do you want to hear me beg for it

   give me more   give me more
  I need more   I can take more

     give it to me I am in love with you
   so open with you   give me more'

then three fingers

 then four

and you were holding my body   rigid
               rift-full

     and I was so aware that you could hold all of me
       all of me at once

danger-less   how healing it was to be in danger-less

as you fucked me I felt myself buckle   open in ways that I have never opened before
  I was choking on my own tears as I struggled to tell you all of this as it was happening

  each shape I saw
  each additional liquid you made in me

dangling
  as the building developed me

    a heaviness that I recognize as what I have had to pass
through in the past
    a heaviness of hybrid corn in ongoing fields
        of lucid memories that are never solid enough to
integrate them
            a heaviness of some inarguable understanding
of ecstasies that relate directly to opened and bloodied robes

        what there is of the sea   left in scenes

        that needed the sea in order to become the sea

I was so riveted by your pressing

"you will never have enough until you have my whole fist inside of you
    you need to be fucked   more deeply than anyone ever
        you are the most expansive

        unendingly expansive"

the way that you put your entire fist inside of me at this point
    with ease   how this entry felt like a harmonic

    struggle-less
        and essential

all at once from everywhere   the feeling of the truth of fullness
came into my body   I felt every pore
I felt every piece of fruit I have ever eaten slowly
I felt every time I have ever needed and not gotten
    every time I have ever been abandoned
      I felt every time I have composed a reach and extended
          I felt the conduction and perpetuation of these
    languages of desire

I felt images as a way of speaking
    I felt the motile-crux

weeping   weeping   weeping
   weeping
    screaming   howling   gripping   grit

    "this is joy   this is joy"

                  then
             silence

    {{{
    {{{
    {{{
    {{{
    {{{{{{{{ (

'when you take me like this I hear the big bang the first sound ever to
    have been heard on this planet   the sound that made
    all other sounds
               and it is the most beautiful thing I could ever
      feel   thank you'
as I reached to be held by you
    'thank you for loving me how I need to be loved'

        and as you wished it to be

           you left me sore with what exists of pleasure

                      far beyond pleasure

000

that there was something specific about that night

        the moonlight juxtaposed against the light of the wildfire

how they both lit the hills

and subatomic anatomies emerged   provoking ether and savors

allowing a continual reflecting on these ohms and strange
    morphologies

        these compressions for the furthering of arousal

continuation as a space

        wrought with answers

                and extensions that relate to nearness

duration

like a sea filled with habitless-ness

           where we weave   uncalled for and unfounded intensities

                    that wait to swallow the earth

plucking sensuous from sumptuous

ensuring

there is no such thing as overstimulation

    if you're continually evolving your body

        to increase its capacity to hold and translate these viscosities

                of the desired force

always something to add to   and adding to

salt for salt

salt on salt

flesh addendums   flesh attenuations

flesh attentions

progressing the questions   and offering these hyperbolas of sop

OOOC

opening the tenses to the position of relief
                                    through the tender reversal of scars

                    eclectic

                    underneath

                                    where we are all haul

this tenderness is a grammar of feeling

like being stung by beauty as recitative

                                    and we come inside of one another

                                    these things that are precious because they are slow

OOOO

from a cosmic womb   or an original vision

to finding new non-dualist ways to womb

so that each touch   each transcended border

each document

       is an augury

              an essential portion of the ultimate oracle

    do my efforts at recording this so relentlessly   prove me as worth?

if my portions seem to be lacking heart or singular lexicon   that is because they supply/offer neither

that is not their project

   they supply figures and shudders   sudden staccatos and slopes

               brutal anatomies

        materialities   mastications

    that once entered by you   you become the heart of

            I am saying that you are essential here

                     to stroke the living into strobes

emanating key proverbs

                    portents and features

with both a subtle panic   and a trust in basic brightness

                                          this longing that is also felt as vertigo

'every time you touch me like this   it is like the first time   it is virginity for me'

you continue   moving me   turning and tilting   exposing then re-covering

'I want to be floating in you   I want you as my oasis
pulling and plucking all of my plumage and carnage forth

I want to be your froth I want to be what you swim in as I come clean'

you take my hand and gently lead me upstairs kiss my fingers and neck   kiss my cicatrix

remove each piece of my clothing   with vital direction

the fact that our conjoined forms make a rounded shape
a mass
the fact that my fantasies are enacted   here   as we eliminate the space between us
here in utter and entire confession

      here in cohesion

      here in full   and genderless

            or gender inventive

      as both atmosphere and ground

      in the same ways that a tea ceremony   enlivens

you lean over me   cover my mouth and eyes   my nose
look at the marks on my body

the remnants of the bruises from where you fucked me last weekend
bites from you
          bites from me   on me   relative to how you made me feel

this is the vitality of the edge

its vials filled with excess and heaving

'I need you so much'

"I see your need   I am going to fuck you   and give you your depth
I am going to make you come and come   and come
          I am going to keep my promises to you   forever"

we feed each other olives that have soaked in vermouth and vodka

covering the body   protecting   with press and reverence

we feed each other one another

you slide into me

relevant

and are watching my face as your hard fills   my eyes cross
my hatches open

      the rain emitting

this is the sound of uninhibited moan

this is a root that is incapable of being silent

I grab your head   then my hands gravitate around your low back
and neck

I pull you into me   from your hips

my lips   quivering   both sets

          sects

::~:::
:::::::~:::::::::::::::::::::::::::::::::::::::~:::::::::::::::::::::::::::::::::::
::::::::::::::::::::::::::~:::::::::::::::::::::::::::::::::::::::~:::::::::::::::::
::::::::::::::::::::::::::::::~::::::::::::::::::::::::~::::::::::::::::::::::::~:::
::::::::::::::::::::~:::::::::::::::::::::

'you feel so good in me this is so primal for me
you   this   fucking   you in me like this
is what I have always been waiting for this is my primal name'

"you're close my baby you're close
              I am gonna do what I want with you
I am gonna make you come"

~:::::::::::::::::::::~:::::::::::::::::::~::::::::::::::::::::::::::::::::~~~~~
:::::::::::::::::::::::::::::::::~~:::::::::::::::::::::::::::::~:::::::::::::::~:::
:::::::::::::::::::~

'how can you tell I am close   whisper it in my ear'

dizzy and sopping
the smell of you   scent embedded in your pores
          your pores embedded in me through this shoving
                              glorious overfill

"I can hear it   I can feel it   your body slows
before you come pounding out with unformed couplets   with
data that has no way of being formulated   it is too beautiful
you are too too beautiful   I am in love with you"

the thrusting of our enjoined lather slows   you grind into me
hips on hips   weight pinned beneath weight

"I need to grab onto the headboard   so I can fuck you
and fuck you   and fuck you"

and you do

we do

me undone through you like this   is my cellularly-accurate tribe

the heritage I will never leave

    the heritage that makes me as it locates me

    which is another way to say

I am suspended in your arms   we splay   we anti-surrogate
through propagation of the deepest variable

        meat   then peppered meat

as an audible site for ensuring

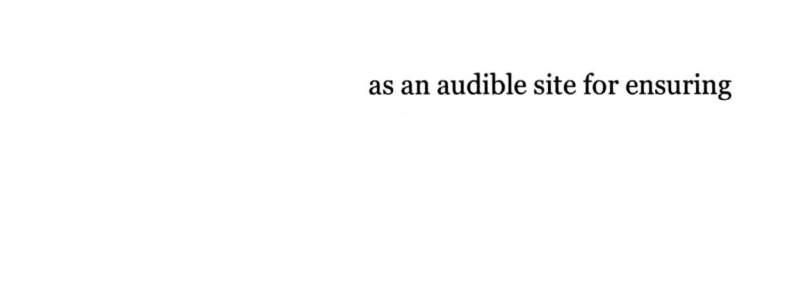

'this is the fucking revolution'

how coil is a centrifugal piece of lace

sealant accruing surge

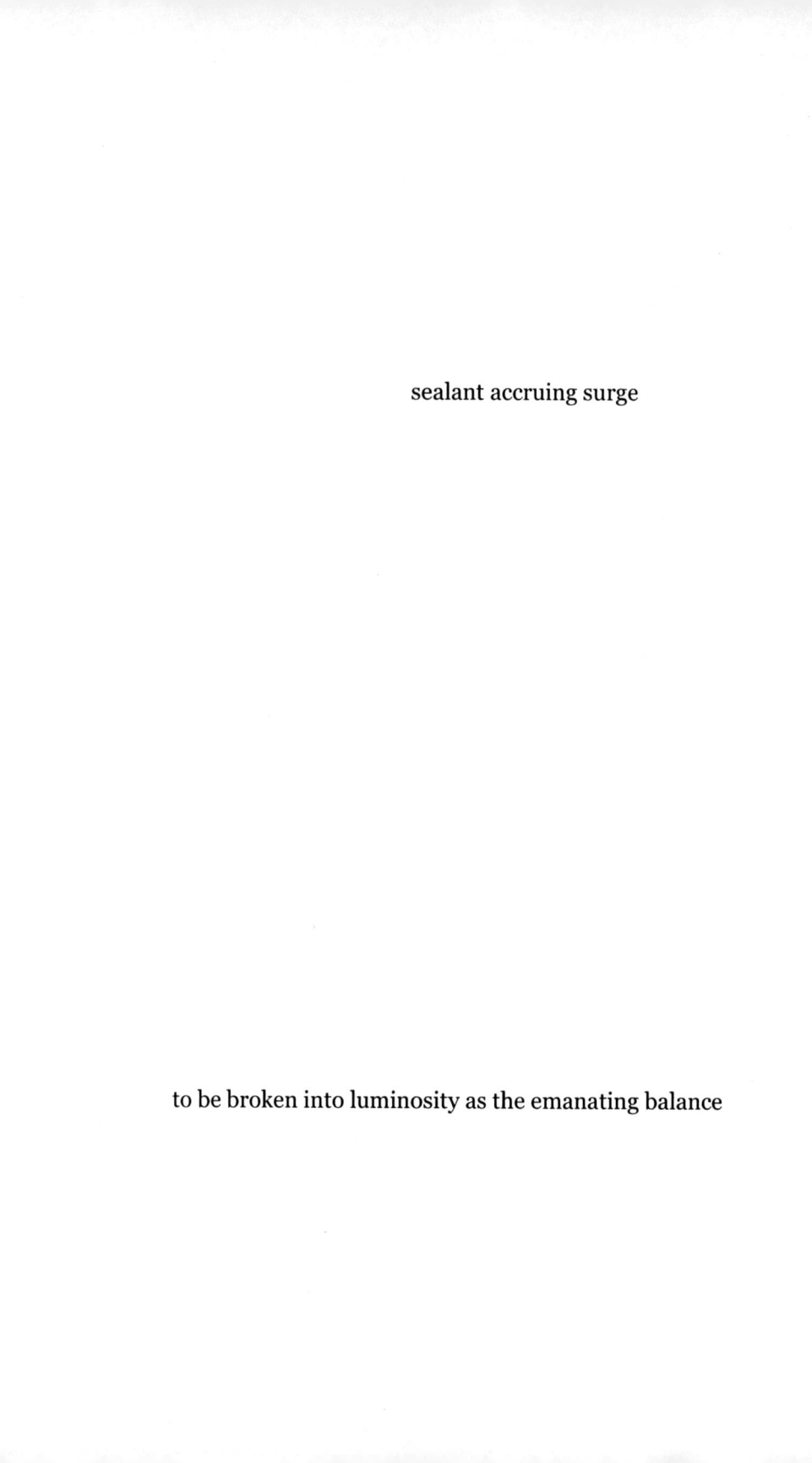

to be broken into luminosity as the emanating balance

transductions of primordial ash

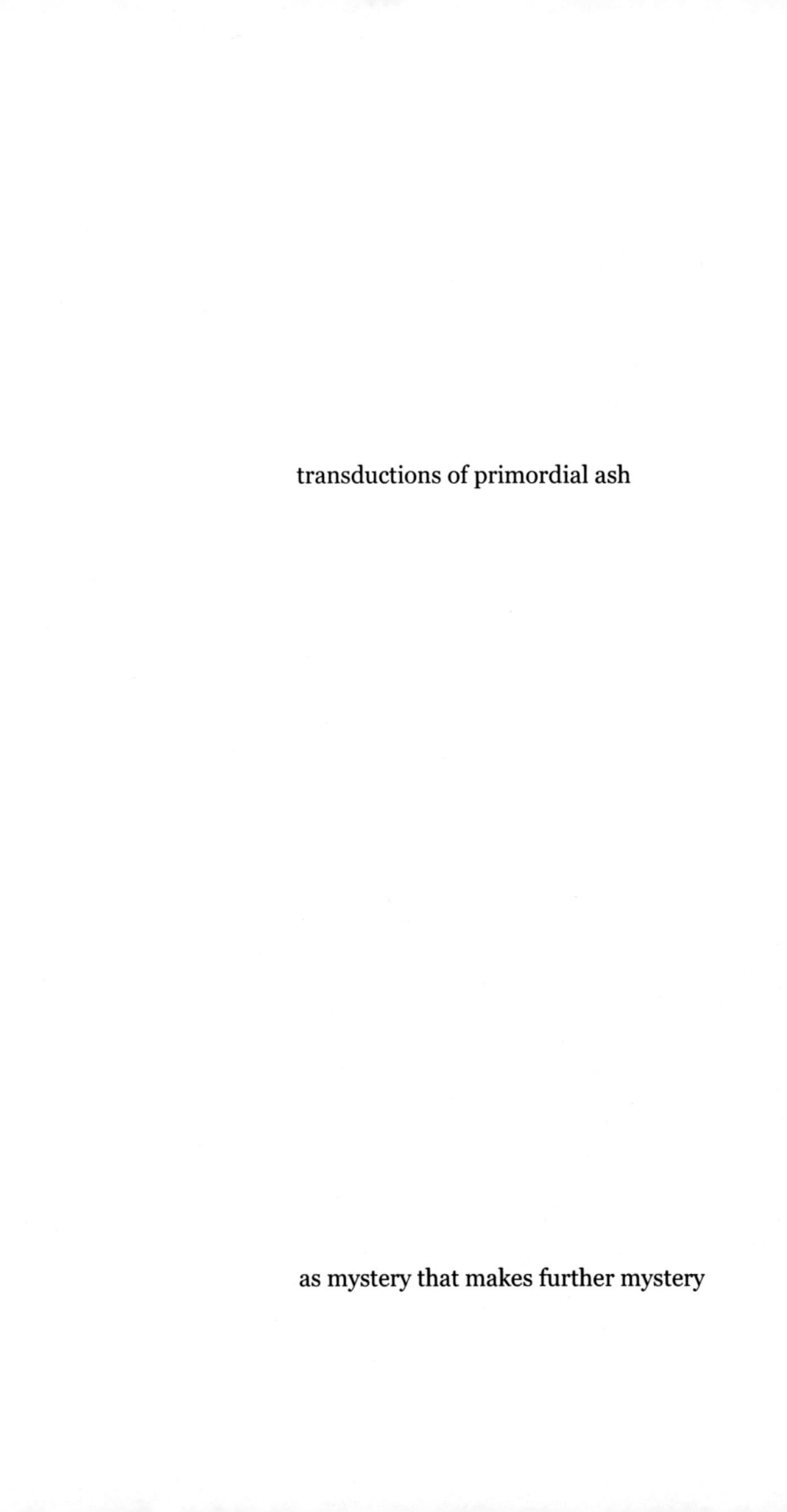

as mystery that makes further mystery

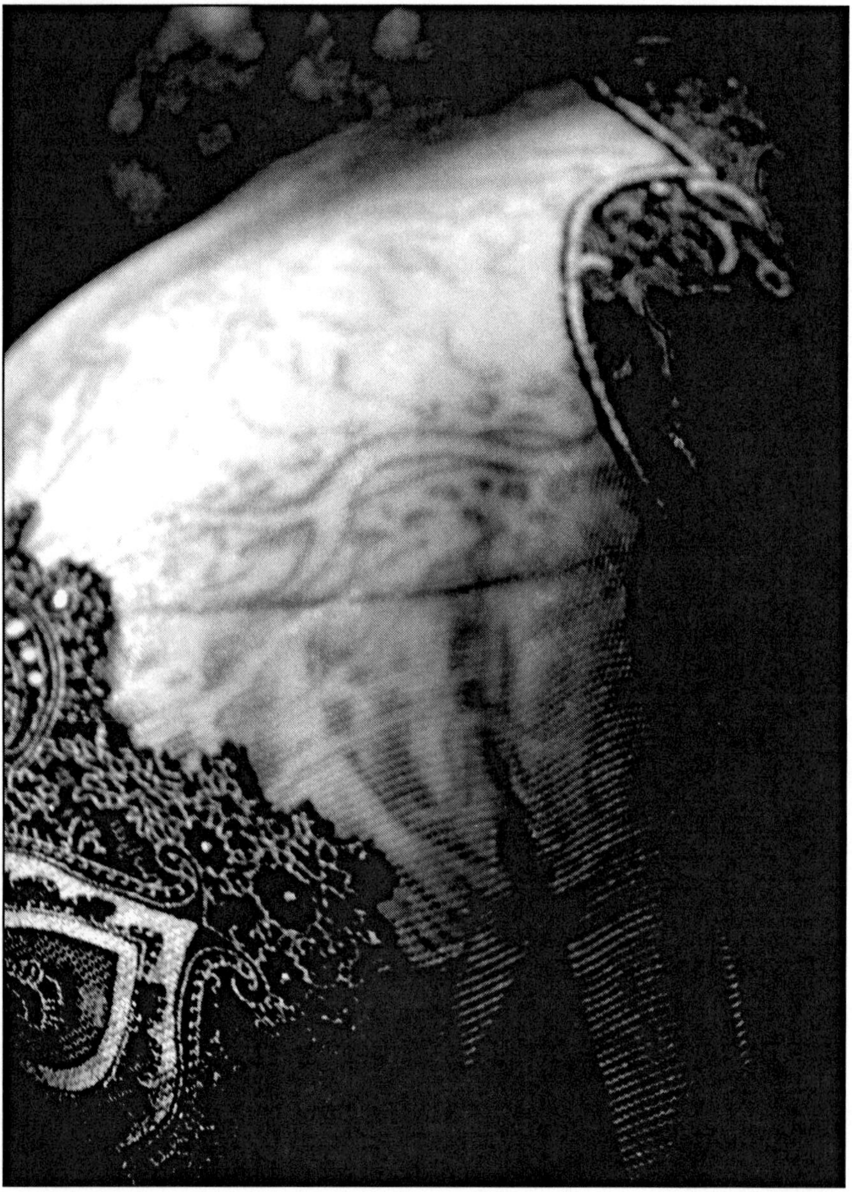

OOOO(

the future of sex is our conjoin

like the sound of the underside of an egret's wings

        all that is being stroked as this listening takes place

            'because everything is sex

                and you are everything I have ever waited for'

we couple our identities
then trivalent them

snagging the fabric in order to see through it

we

        collating and collaborating the supernumerary instant

                each brutal and vital technology for   loving

       it is true that the only thing one has to do for their entire life

          is find the quaking sites for their own accurate slippage

                then populate those sites with vehemence

                        as distended

                              as thread-borough

                    and 'all of the ways I wish to hail you'

this   in order to be met

   always   in order to be met

has there ever been a book   that exists as a direct ongoing
document of sex?

sex as space
           where it both makes the logic

               as well as sustains it?

this is that book

this is that puja

OOOOO

we ecstasy as a verb
        by building these maxima*** systems of shape and touch

allowing reoccurring contact with the streaming

       with cyborg sperm and iridescent wills

                chewing and extending as bodies of quill

                    that appear just out of reach

                        until together

                            we clutch

sureness that continues to enact our interiorities
                            as an exposed will

                      like saints who can and must

explicit praise as we bow prostrate before

        the phallus   ::::::::::   an applicable shape

                      not as a possession of the male's

'what makes a thing truly beautiful?'

        brilliances of personal desire

        the fossa   :::::::::   an applicable shape

                      not as a possession of the female's

this is how we obliterate binary

        these are vellum versions of a magpie

                in a stripped but never blank sky

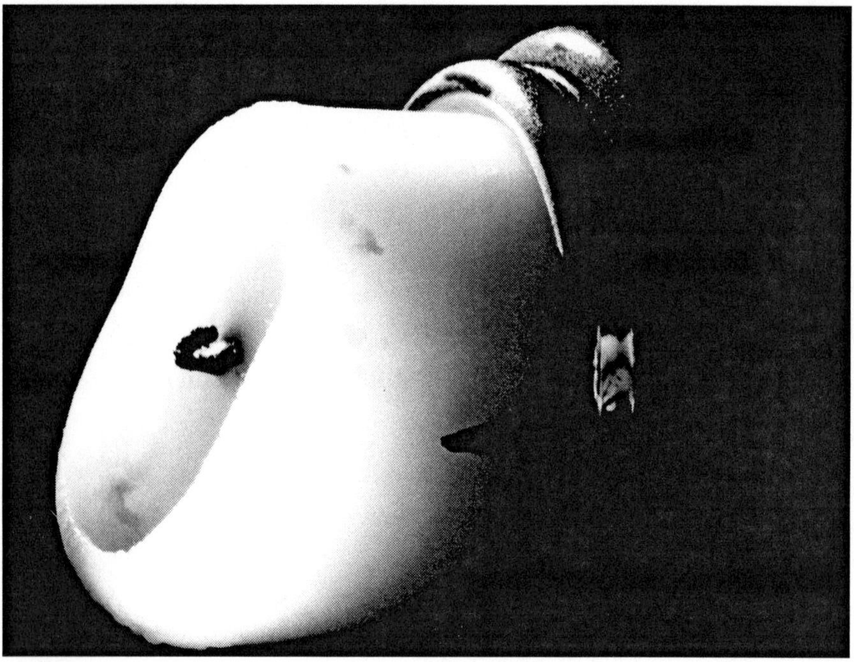

OOOOO(

there is a continual need for gesture here

                                        because waiting halts halos

so together   we hunt

meter and cannon

        overlapping gushes

                              and vivacity cocoons

it has to do with how the shape shifts
                                      once we've implanted bounce in it

to be rescued
        revived
                resuscitated

the slow construction of these nomenclatures

                                                for our coy-radiance

OOOOOO

'you make me feel like I have beehives in my body'

the sudden explosive progressions of a star

    or skin-nautilus successively

      mortar and cleave as the model

          for our future based in the forever fleshenizing

                                        all parts and ports poised as alternates
                                        to stasis

                                        entangled with emollient

                                                          as emollient

slowly learning   to eat the space between us

      these terms of the felt-totem

      to increase the liquid at all costs

::~:::
:::
:::
:::
::::::::::::::::::::::::::::::::~~

to increase the liquid at all costs

OOOOOO(

'I love our positions'

the myriad

       where revision occurs as a natural reaction to continuance

       through allowing our viscous compatibilities to seep   as overt

       through becoming entirely one another's

       on every plane of design

                                in every type of time

[~~[

the sensation of having come to the complete edge   of a curve

marinating then sautéing boundaries
that were once shaped and are now shaping

the past is   ::~:: 'I want to speak to your yet to be
disclosed/s ravaging'

locations that now maintain their own reflections without effort
because they have given everything
because they have been given everything

a cut red crayon
against textures of estrogen and testosterone

sweet chemical inductions that lead to alchemical drifts

what is it to supplant the eye for the sake of its futures?

what is light as that action's recuperation?

we   the provokers of descant   and aperture

what is emotional surgery?

what happens to the motile body if it finds a home?

creaming   rhombus

'in you   in you'

I am admittedly constructing these skins without a formula
to vibrate and make amaranthine through their ascensions and
dissents

in order to make a life that is living me into meaning
through matter   fusing with its others

and thus itself

to love is to open one's mouth to the world
to the wars
to the desperations
to the contours

'I have been waiting my entire existence for you
to climb me
to add me

to re-invent me and thereby make me real'

    to transfer the borders into amalgamated areas
       due to due to

'I don't fit any contagion of pronouns

      I am ice soaked in black-salts

I   most deeply identify

       as both conjure

        and yours

   I am saying I am most at home

        in you'

there is no such thing as redundancy in this shaping

because awe is   allowing your body to go

all of the places it craves going

into/as the tundra of its yearnings

that it is through this allowance   that ease truly begins :: ~

its stirs

OOO:OOO

oh plethora   where we ensure these pleats

making the solid cylinder transparent

    or the transparent cylinder solid

        as granulates in the capitulation

in order to guarantee these dictionaries of beauty

    'I am occupied here'

    and our co-avenue is slowly composed

        of quaking

        you suck on my ear

            whisper-heat

    and so appears

    a celestial stomach

    a glottal unearthing

        a material splendor of slicks

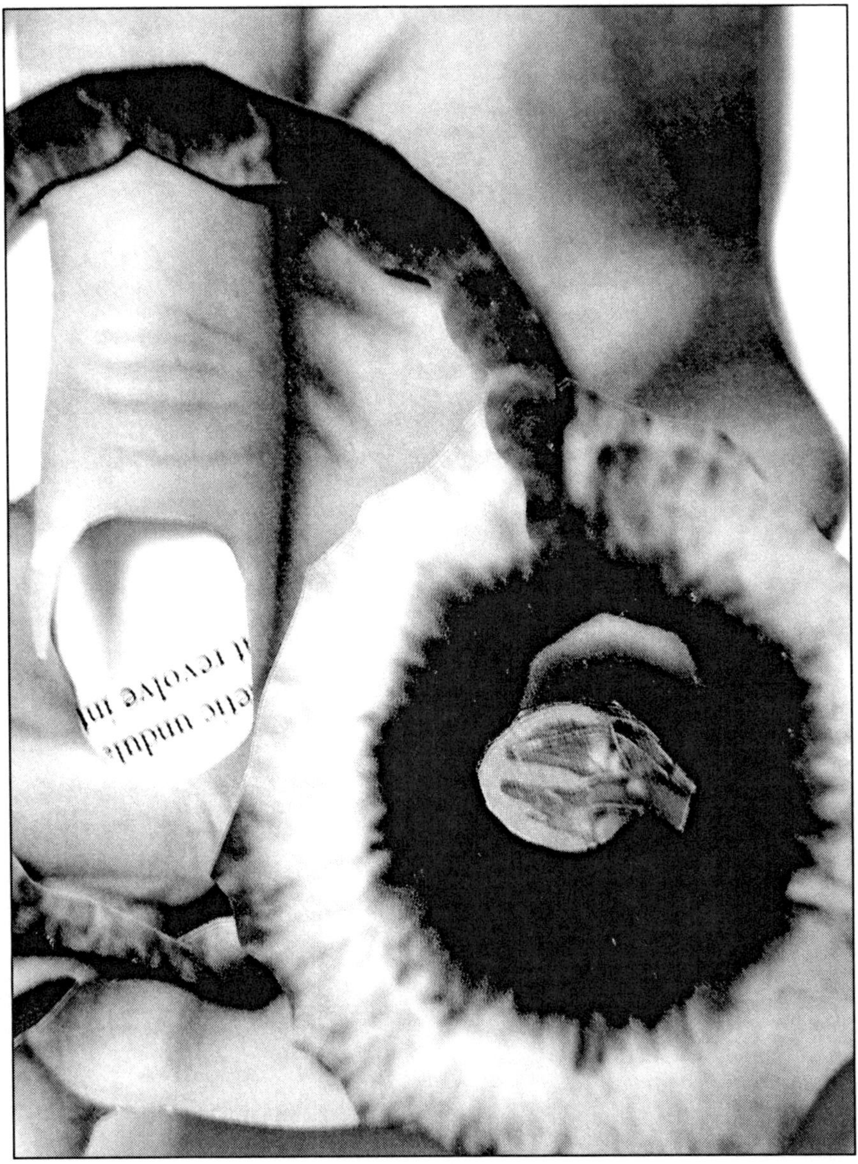

0~000~0(

where is the memory of the increases that stain   the body

       as it relates to these types of questions?

                                 monotone-less

       elucidating our place in eternity   as eternity we make it rotatable   going into the sea with our mouths open

to learn what is retained when no form is imposed   on what could naturally gather

and provide ulterior vision to

                              thereby learning how it feels when no hood is applied

we make ourselves stay   abyssmal

            long enough to remember   and retain

                        what was never conceived of

                                    until now

OOOOO

there is complication in this

    there is post-lude

        locality and rogue ethics

            how we are a path that is also a bruise

                    because we remain

everything that is ever made   is a devoted map of the key

which is not neutral

nor is it designed to solve

the infrared umbra that leads us

as its centrifugal nomads

inverting umbrellas   if only to catch and somehow preserve

the tears

                                                      turns

                                                                                   and clandestine theatres

opening   gaping

with funnels attached to each of our pores

      to ensure pour

                            dew that is comprehended as honey

digging into my body for pleasure and tidal release

in the same ways that you whisk me across a dance floor

          this is emotional dna meeting capacity

                   as the body continues   slackened

your eyes like two distinct tigers

their jaws filled with lilies as they mount

0O~::~0O(

        nude-melodic

        we move to the floor

        and lay there

        nurturing this inertia

I notice how mature you feel as you take   like this
how noble and responsible

and how much this allows me to release further

'so round in the middle but it spins'

"you are my god"

        as we fold   all types   of surrounding atmosphere

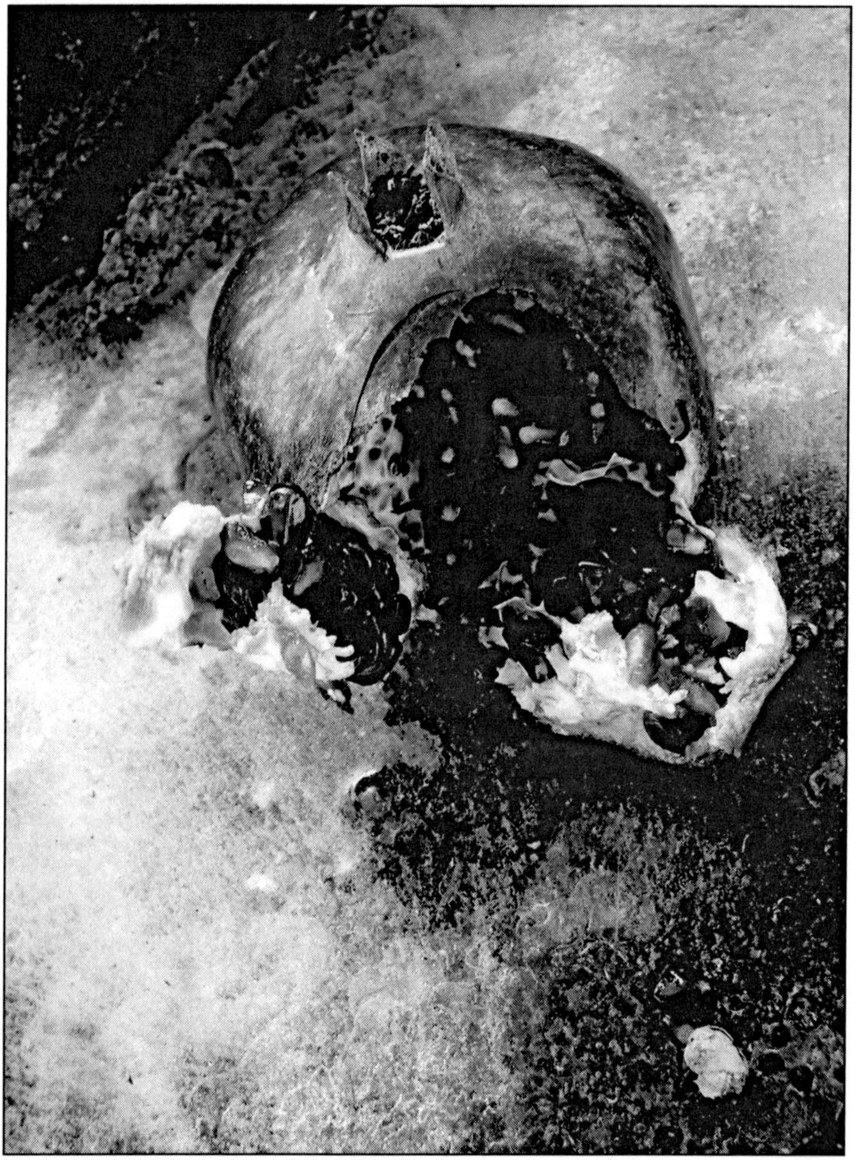

00[~~[0(

to

:::::::::::::::::::::

the compiler of Romeos   feral stallions

and other syncopated-plights

I was never destined to be a biography of compliances

so instead   these untamed vestibules

          vistas

                    with accuracies and fullnesses

                              as its venture

                                    as its unequivocal name

promulgating exertions throughout each dominant interlude

operating as new types of bounty that lead us to

lineless

grace

all of the principles involved in vivisecting

these superlative bodies   boldly

0O=0(((((

meaning is encouraged to occur interactively

                with imperative   viscous hopes

making inebriated scenes and crushed seams

      connotation-shores

           making new threads and natures

                as the unwavering freedom in our mills

::
::
::::::::::::::::::::::::::::::::::::.*.::
::.*.::::::::::::::::::~:::::::::::::::::::::
:::::::::::~:::

this is a flexing confession   bulbous with
its hinges and qualities of decay

       ever complexing and flexing   the Beloved

as a bruised palette becoming recognized

                              becoming familiar

        as a concertina caught in and ever adding to

                  vortex

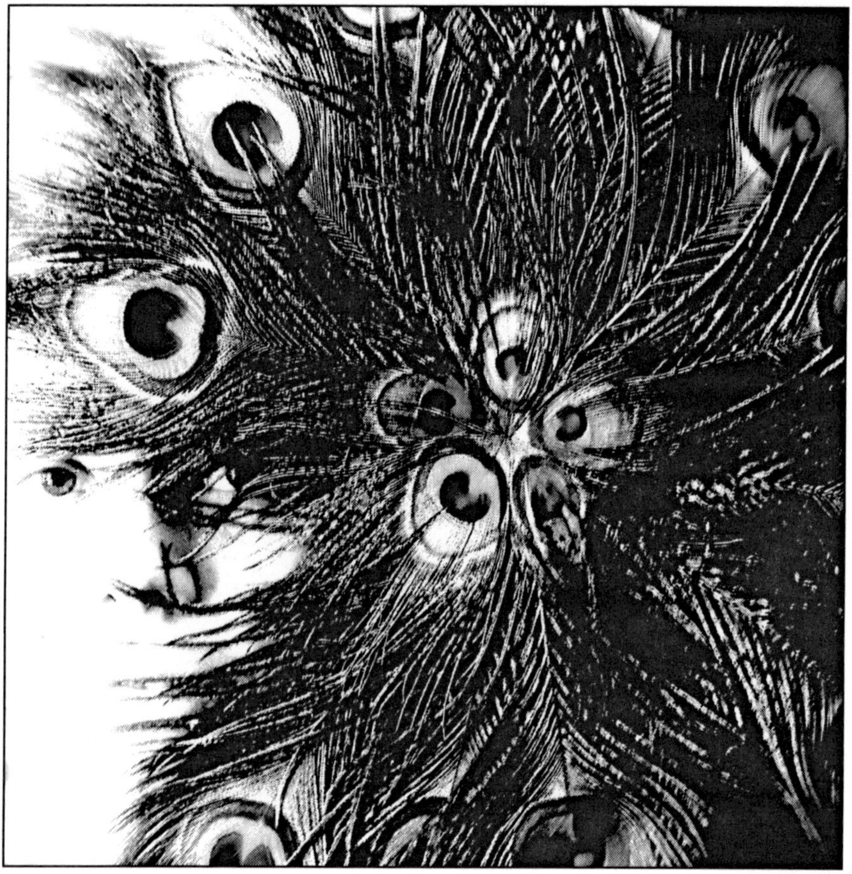

(~   ~   ` `   ~~~~~

there was the brim   the need to focus   on the feeling
of your fist
inside of

this was fullness so true   that without stretch   it would have
resulted in tearing

because I need in the most pungent   raw   exposed forms

        where avatar and brusque tonalities commune

                              these are the hand extracted

                                      messages

                                            the initiation

un-sewing the notion of cage

we rouse

       implanting animateness as analysis

              in place of anything that was once felt like a prison

*~::::::::::::::::::::::::

there is neoteric beauty in this emotional/spiritual excavation

      where induction is seen as a form of non-redundant

                                                                                fluency

you bend me over a brick wall   enter me   enthrone

                            these styles in use

this is the feeling that I am always trying to say

        and I am unable to feel it without you

something like reep   reaping   grow

                            then the vivacious hewing stem that follows it

oh sensory endocrine

these are fugues that must be noticed

                                        this is why and how we have come so far

                                                          I offer you the pillow

                amidst a great greased slot dangling from the sky

                        a slot that is slowly being filled

                            with these songs compiled from

                                        storages of the slippage and the silt

this is healing beyond itself

                        as neon yearn-cells are being swathed into

                    globular   resuscitations

which take place   only past true alliance and allegiance   toward

                                                       fluidly
                                                       episodic

              how inter-elocution

                    is ultimately what makes

                            the text   and our enjoined bodies

                                  electric

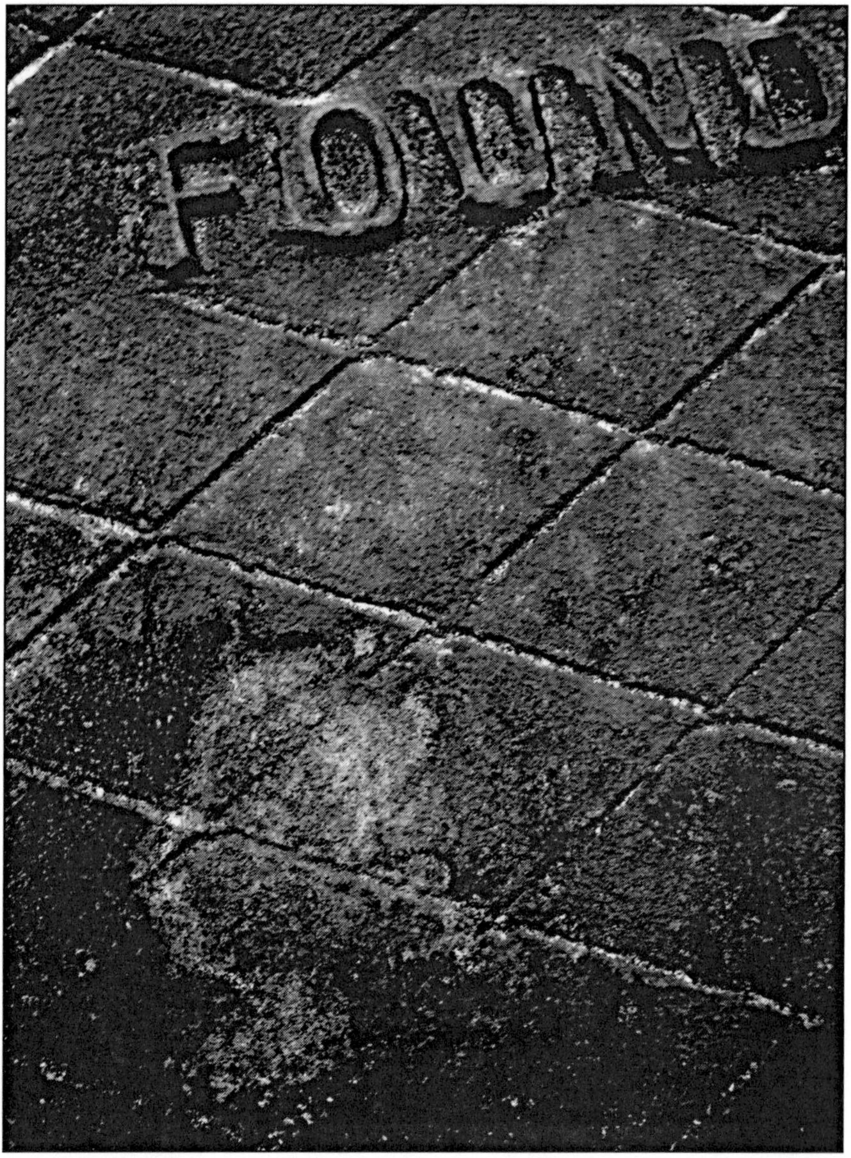
FOUND

Biographical Note

j/j hastain is currently living and writing in Colorado. j/j is the author of the full-length book *asymptotic lover // thermodynamic vents* (BlazeVox 2008) and chapbooks *poetics of merge* and *'my body as your trance'* (Arsonesque Press 2007), *.compilate.* (Livestock Editions 2008) and *the let me letters* (soon to come out with Pudding House Publications). j/j's writing has appeared in numerous journals including MiPoesias, and the hotmetalpress Poetry prize of 2008.

j/j received a BA in poetry, music, gender and cultural studies, and an MFA in contemporary poetics.

j/j defines as trans (which is different than transgendered, though not at all discounting it). j/j is interested in the differentiated usages of the prefix trans (when it is utilized in ways that are not at all related to previously determined models (with binary derived bases) of identity construction. j/j's life work involves embodying, inhabiting and populating the body as one would a neoteric space—through ways and methods that are not related to formerly prescribed shapes that are based in limit.

contact j/j at: www.jjhastain.com